cold outside,
warm inside,
and warmer still
inside our stillness.

come morning
you & I discovered we
and the snow
had fallen
in love.

outside
we will build a snowman
and a relationship
and love it
until it melts.

Jai

Guru

Dev

evolving at the speed of Love

for Clare.

see how you are?

the enclosed poems,
printed here in the order
in which they were written,
will hopefully give you a
thumbnail sketch of
a love,
as it evolved and dissolved.

where are you
that I could find you?

Here am I
that you can find me.

and if we never meet,
Know that I love you.
I know you love me.

I may be ready
around the next corner,
I may be writing
around the next page
waiting
to touch you.

fal
l
l
l
l
l
l
l
l
l
l
ing in love

fal
l
l
l
l
l
l
l
l
l
ling at the rate
of 33 feet
per second
per second.

hel
l
l
l
l
l
l
l
l
l
lp

thud.

ouch.

oh.
this one is
going to
hurt.

I am
falling faster
than I said
I would
or thought
I could.

and you aren't
helping any.

you're so
comforting
&
creative
&
beautiful
&
full filling

I am falling.
I will flap my arms
and pretend to be flying.

help me.
break my
    fall.
catch me
        with your smile.

I don't want to love you
too much.
I don't want you to hate me.

I want the
relation ship
to sail around the world
on calm, sun-lit waters.

I do not want to sink
another vessel on the
sea of my inner storm

care full.

I destroy those I love.
Like you.

I even destroy those I
don't
love.
        like me.

can you feel my soul
turn its face to God
and smile as you touch
my chest   so

or maybe it's my heart
smiling at my love for

your soul turning to God
or your heart turning to
love

or your hand turning to
touch my face

facing my love;
feeling my God;

facing my god;
feeling my love feel me

                    so.

how can I
no
one so wonderful?

how can I
know
one so complex?

yes, do, touch me.

yes, please, love me.

I will respond
spontaneously
and love & touch
in return.

I know I will want
to touch
when you are gone.

and I will
love
as you give your
wonders to another.

in that
Impossible Moment
I will write the world
a memorandum,
sharing my sorrow
with fellow fatalities.

but tonight
I will enjoy
your
smile
    &
        touch
           &
               words
                   &
                       love.

and maybe you will
surprise me and spend
a week.

and maybe you will
shock me and spend
a month.

and maybe you will
put me in a coma
and spend a life.

but I will not think of
beginnings or endings now.

only of your
               soft
                   soft
                       soft

there you were

and I was moved

and you made the first move

and I was shocked

and you wanted to move in

and I was flabergasted

and here you are

and I am happy

hello.

Did I tell you
that I love you?

Maybe I was
too busy
loving
to tell.

but I can tell.

now.

I can tell me.

and,
being 500 miles away,
I can even tell
you.

remember that sculpture
of the figure with
the hole in its stomach?

that's what I feel like.

my stomach is experiencing
labor pains. It is about
to give birth to my love
for you. my body has
anesthetized the
entire area. I
can't feel my
stomach
at all.

would you?

my feeling for you
has main offices
in my head
    my chest
& my loins.

it has regional
and branch offices
everywhere else,
and is seeking further
room for
e x p a n s i o n

missing you

could turn from

pain
to
pleasure

if only I knew

you

were missing me

too

i need food
i need sleep
i need meditation
i need activity.

i like you,
but i do not
need you. yet.

if you could find
a place to live
within the space
between the needs,
I would like you
more.

Perhaps you would
become a fifth need.

in our first week together
why did I never say

I Love You. ?

I had the time
and the inclination
and the environment.

I even had the receptivity,
which is the rarest of all.

why didn't I.

I want to now,

but this is our week
apart.

and who can express love
in a letter?
            it comes off
sounding like a contract
rather than a feeling.

Oh, but I do love you.

can you feel it?

all those miles,

       can I warm you?

I want to
I want you
I love you
I need you
I miss you
I   you

       hurry.

       I have something
       to tell you
       when you
       return

the fine line between
helping
and
hindrance
is a hard one to walk;

especially with you.

your life seems full of
people who try to bind
you to them with their
Good Advice.

the next time I try to
offer you some "good advice"
give me some:

                    shut up.

filling
holes,
becoming
whole.

attempting
to be
worthy
of
each others
caress.

evolving
at the
speed
of
love.

I missed you last night.
I missed you this morning.
I meditated.
I no longer miss you.
I love you.

be
in
g.

first
I have to get
        out
of love with you.

second
I have to remember

don't fall
until you see
the whites
of their
lies

you left
traces
of your self
all over my room

a poem scribbled in the
margin of a book.

a corner of a page
turned over in another book.

your smell on my blanket.

where are you tonight.

in whose room are you leaving
traces.

are you maybe
discovering
the traces of my self
I left on your soul.

went out today
on a
busy-ness trip.

I wheeled and dealed
and smiled & beguiled
and got all I wanted.

I returned home to
find I had missed
a long distance
phone call from
you.

the trip was a failure.

I don't want
to build my
life around
you,

but I want to
include you
in the building
of my life.

I came to see you,
not the ocean.

I came to be with you,
not sea gulls.

I came to communicate with you,
not nature.

When I stare at a scene
worthy of a full color
picture postcard

I contemplate your navel

come,
spend a year and a night
with me.

come,
denounce the world
pronounce the word
                    love.

come,
be my daily motivation,
my nightly activity.

come,
evolve with me.
revolve with me around
                          we

come,
be.

come,
be
come
my
One

you are too good
what you are today.

you are to good
what sun is to May.

I am too. good.
what I am to stay.

we are, too good,
what I mean to say.

to open myself
to the happiness of
    us
is also subjecting
    I
to the hurtfullness of
    you.

as much as I need to
    love
is as much as I can't stand to
    hate.

as much as I want
    joy,
to that degree I cannot tolerate
    pain.

I know that perhaps I
should pause and wait,

but I am too lonely.

how do I love thee?
let me count the lays.

although you are the
finest one thus far,

for the first time I feel
I would rather live
my life
alone.

than

your life
together.

so I can understand your
going,

but I wish you weren't.

and I realize why you are
leaving,

I realize, too, my hurt.

I can't live with you.
I won't let it happen.

I cannot place my
total vulnerability
in such insensitive hands.

I will place my hands
on your sensitive body
and make myself
physically vulnerable,

but my soul will not be moved.

it will be encased in a
plexiglass shrine until
you have fled my temple.

only then will it come out
and smell the air and warm
my body left cold by your
inevitable departure.

leave my life
        quickly

as quickly as you came.

give me pain and desolation
as quickly and intently as
you gave love and lust.

don't let me
fall   a   part.

go
leaving a crumpled me
            &
no forwarding address

I do alright
alone
and better
together
but
I do very poorly
when
semi-
together.

in solitude
I do much
in love
I do more
but
in doubt
I only transfer
pain to paper
in gigantic Passion Plays
complete with miracles and martyrs
and crucifixions and resurrections.

come to stay
or
stay away.

this series of passion poems
is becoming a heavy cross to bare.

how I
love you and hate you.

how bound I am to you.
how bound I am to break my bondage.

I want to be free!

I want to be able to
enjoy the day again

and give me back my nights.

I do not want to
let myself feel
the fear
within me.

I fear it too much.

I do not want to
let myself feel
the pain
within me.

I do not know
how deep
it goes

or how much
of my love
for you it will
destroy.

you like it that I write
poems
about you.

your ego takes some
perverse pleasure
in them.

you will cause
enough pain to fill
a book, and then
send autographed
copies to your
friends.

clouds ingest the moon.

raindrops die with a
splat on concrete causeways.

the floodgates are about to burst.

I wish you were gone
and when you go
I wish you are here.

a banchee howls
over our love.

I will never have a love
    but
I will never realize this.

It's always
    you & you & you
but it's really
    me.

I'll try again
and gain again
and die again
and push on into the night.

to be reborn by a
look and a touch.
and to hope again that
this time it will last
and to know
it will not be the last.

my one gnawing need
is the need to be touched

embraced
          caressed
                    physically loved
          coddled
fondled

to be known
to share secrets
to pain
to talk
to see the world

all these are secondary
to the reality of touch

come.
come.

such a wonderous word.

come.

so many meanings.
and each meaning
meaning full.

come.
come.

not turned trite
by the abuse of overuse
as
"beautiful"
"together"
and
"love"
         have.

come.

I hope Mass Media
and Madison Avenue
never discover you . . .

but I hope every body
else does.

         come.

colors are brighter
since you've come to
stay a while.

my heart beats in time
with the universal
song of love.

loneliness . . . pain . . .
where are you hiding,
my long time comrades?

maybe they have gone
where you came from,

and they will no doubt
return
when you do.

where we are
has no words.

so why do I
keep trying to
write about
It.

how long will you stay this time

I ask.

an unfair question

you respond.

an unfair answer

I reply.

Did I love you?
yes.

Do I miss you?
yes.

Did you love me?
well.

Does it hurt me?
well . . .

it was good, and
"all good things
must come to an end."

I learned that
a long time ago.

maybe now I am just
beginning to
Know
it

I think about you
entirely too much
while you're away.

when you're here
these thoughts I call
"love".
when you're not,
a less flattering term
comes to mind.

If only I was sure.
sure that you wanted
to be back as much as
I want you back.

that would help.
or,

sure that you didn't really
want to come back at all.

that would help too.

but I'm not sure.
not certain.
not happy.
alone.
in love
with you.

on my back
in the dark
speaking freely of my fears
of we.

emotions, made of words,
hang suspended in mid air.

I finish.
I wait.
I listen.
I hope
you will take the fears
and give me rest.

silence.

fear floats near the ceiling
and mingles with the air awhile.

a sound:
you rolling over,
falling asleep.

the fear
slowly descends and crushes me
in the dark.

with solitude comes the loneliness that makes me long for you. with you comes the pain that makes me long for solitude.

how do I count on thee?
let me love the ways.

having you here
was problems.

having you gone
is pain.

the fear that I would
come home one day and
find you gone has turned
into the pain of the
reality.

"What will I do if it happens?"
I would ask myself.

What will I do
now that it
has
?

angry but silent and
walking away

this will be your last
memory of me.

hitching and freezing
in an autumn rain.

this will be your last
memory of Michigan.

I hope Atlanta or New Orleans
or San Francisco will be
warmer to you this winter
than I could have been.

I know it was time for us
to part,

but today?

I knew I had much pain to
go through,

but tonight

?

I hope you find a friend.

I was yours.

I hope you find a love.

You were mine.

The Books of Peter McWilliams

Come Love With Me And Be My Life

I Have Loved

For Lovers And No Others

I Loved Therefore I Am

The Hard Stuff: Love

Evolving At The Speed of Love

**Available from your local
Bookmonger or directly from:**

℣ersemonger Press
**5806 Elizabeth Court
Allen Park, Michigan 48101**